What Readers Are Saying:

"Awesome read that draws you in from the beginning. Pressing to be authentically ME! Life altering."

"This reality check, as I call it, will have you soul searching and seeking ways to overcome your insecurities, intimidations, doubt, know your self-worth, be the you God intended you to be, and be alright with it."

"Simply amazing!! What a wonderful work of literature, compassion, insight, and transparency. It is a book for ANYONE who's DOING SOMETHING."

"As I read, I took a journey of self-discovery and now I'm ready to do the work to heal! Thank you for sharing your thoughts to help others know they are not alone."

OTHER BOOKS BY AUTHOR

Nanny Nuggets

When He Whispers

When Life Speaks

And It Is So

MASTERS
OF THE
MASK

Andrea L. Hines

Studio Griffin
A Publishing Company
www.studiogriffin.net

For information, contact:
Studio Griffin
A Publishing Company
studiogriffin@outlook.com
www.studiogriffin.net

Cover Design by Ruth E. Griffin
Image by © GulyaevStudio / Adobe

First Edition

ISBN-13: 978-1-954818-40-8

Library of Congress Control Number:
2023935568

1 2 3 4 5 6 7 8 9 10

I would love to acknowledge every conversation with every individual who contributed to the content of this labor of love. However, that would be another book with another title in and of itself. The concept was developed over a long period of time as I did my own soul searching and took a front row seat to watch the lives of others play out before me. Some endings were amazing; others proved that, more often than not, our perception of happily ever after was a rarity. Whether life produced a standing ovation or premature lowering of the curtain there were certain similarities that could not or should not be ignored. Discover them in these pages, enjoy them, learn from them and when you take center stage, get ready for your curtain call!

INTRODUCTION

Who are you? I know that might seem an odd way to begin, but before you answer, I really want you to stop for a moment and think about your life and how you live it. Sounds like a pretty tall order and perhaps it might be. Most of us would like to believe we are the same way all the time, no matter where you see us and no matter what we are doing. If you can do that successfully, I applaud you; I really do. While some of us may come close, I believe we all have little nuances that cause us to become slightly different depending upon the role we play, the hat we wear, and the mask we choose to hide behind.

For example, women have taken on the role of provider which puts them in places in corporate America, or as business owners or those having an entrepreneurial spirit. They are taking care of themselves and their families at much different levels than they did 'back in the day.' They are entering new career paths and that means new responsibilities. Different doors are opening in just about every industry. Different roles create different requirements and different requirements mean different mindsets in order to navigate from one role to another.

Let me first clarify that I am not a mental health professional by any stretch of the imagination, but I do care about humanity. I'm just someone tired of watching people self-destruct from trying to be what they think other people want them to be and losing sight of who they are. I'm saddened by people whose lives end too soon because they didn't feel they could seek help, and when and if they did, they were met with ridicule which led to embarrassment and shame. I am saddened as I watch the suicide numbers climb seemingly every year. I believe that there is something we can do, if nothing more than adjusting our thinking on life and how we live it.

In today's time, it is politically correct (for lack of a better term) to talk about 'living in your truth.' I've found that real truth requires transparency and trust, neither of which opens the door to a place and space that is automatically safe and comfortable. It often unlocks the doors to pain and scars you'd rather hide than heal. And how can we deal with vulnerability that we perceive, if exposed, will make us weak? If we don't have the strength to navigate the journey, we will be taken advantage of, misused, and abused. So we build walls and we hide behind half-truths or whatever mechanism is at hand believing it is safer to conceal rather than reveal. It can become a proposition that is risky business, often-times leading to dangerous outcomes.

When you begin to have internal struggles and start to tire of the facade something has to change. That person people think they see has become your representative, not who you really are. When presenting that person becomes more important than loving the person God designed you to be, the results can manifest in ways that will cause self-destruction and self-sabotage through addictive behaviors, alcoholism, drug abuse, eating disorders, depression, mental illness, and suicidal thoughts. We want everyone to think we have it all together, and we don't. We want everyone to think we are in control, and we're not. We don't want to admit we need help, and we do. And heaven forbid we share the details of who we really are and what it really takes for us to make it through the day with the right person, and we should.

We are talking more and more about being healthy and whole. I get that and I'm on board. I guess that's why I think it's important to shed some light on this, if only the flame of a match. I'm not sure when we reached a point of thinking we could handle what feels like the weight of the world and still be okay. Hiding the real you is a heavy responsibility that will eventually affect you mentally and physically. It's like living at the masquerade ball, having worn a mask so much it becomes a part of you, and you don't know what to do without it.

This is not necessarily a comfortable topic to bring under the spotlight. However, I think it is one worth exploring or inspecting on whatever level you choose. Depending on where you look or who you ask, the primary areas of your life fall into different categories and the numbers vary from four to twelve. They include everything from health to relationships and all things in between. Sometimes they are referred to as areas of importance, or keys, perhaps even levels to life. Whatever you choose to call them, for the purpose of my observation and discussion, I think the trio of the hats, roles, and masks fall into four major categories. I feel they are worthy of our consideration, at the very least, because these are the places we are most likely to be chameleons. We shift our opinions and behaviors according to the situations and ease in our ability to hide in plain sight. But before we get into the different areas, let's begin at the beginning and answer the first question. Who are you?

THE MAN IN THE MIRROR TAKES CENTER STAGE

All the world's a stage and all the men and
women merely players.
They have their exits and their
entrances and one man in his time
plays many parts.
William Shakespeare
(As You Like It)

I recently spent some time looking over my life, where I've been, where I am today and how I got to this point. Of course, I discovered some things. Some were a surprise, and some were expected. When you do a checkup in the mirror, clean the mirror, and take a good hard look at the reflection staring back at you. There's a lot that goes through your mind at that moment. At least it did for me. What happened to the little girl, the young lady, the wife, the divorcee? Where did she go? And the partying, chain smoking IBM executive—how and when did she disappear? How did I go from just going to church to passionately serving in His house? How did I go from Sister Hines to Elder, to an Honorary Doctorate in Divinity, how? And let's not even begin to unveil the portrait of the 'family you' versus the 'professional you.' That's an entirely different story.

To get a baseline for this journey I really want you to stop, as I did, and think about your life and how you live it. Introspection and self-assessments can be wonderful things if you are willing to do the work, and then work on the outcome.

I opted to take center stage and make the

'man in the mirror' the foundational layer that everything comes from or is built around. My belief is each one of us has been placed in the earth, hand crafted and God designed for a specific purpose. You know the scripture in Psalm 139...

'fearfully and wonderfully made...'

However, you have to know who you are created to be in order to know when you have changed or made adjustments to handle the vicissitudes of life. Many people take pride in being the jack of all trades. They don't mind being cook, housekeeper, business owner, mom, dad, committee chair, prayer partner, etc. They take pride in being sought after as all things to all people, especially when there is a critical need. You become the 'go to' person. Great. Grand. Wonderful. Until you have nothing left to give and begin to wonder, "How did I get myself into this…?"

Every area of my life I mentioned has required something different from me. I never wanted to lose myself in trying to fulfill the assignments and situations where I found myself. While I had to adjust it didn't mean I had to make a complete metamorphosis, but some people do. Subtle changes in how you carry yourself, your conversation, etc. come about depending on, not only what is required of you, but who you are around. It gets tricky when you become an award-winning thespian in the play of your life, The 'professional you' does not recognize the 'social you' when you let your hair down. The 'social you' doesn't recognize the 'family you' at the football game. The 'family you' doesn't recognize the 'church you' at the food pantry. The 'church you' doesn't really know who you are beyond the Praise the Lord standard greeting in the four walls of the spiritual house.

I never wanted or expected to play so many roles, wear so many hats, fulfill so many assignments. When you do, it is not unreasonable to ask the question. How do I keep it all together, so no one realizes I am falling apart? Having a lot on your plate can often take its toll. You have to have a balance in your life. What you do shouldn't change who you are at your core but sometimes it does. We want to do well; we want to be well thought of; we want to be informed; we want to be successful at whatever we're doing and acknowledged favorably by whomever we are around. We want to believe we can be our best selves no matter what and not be influenced by the opinions of those around us. That would be great if we didn't fall into the trap somewhere along the line of believing we're responsible for making sure everything and everyone around us is safe, happy, well adjusted, and has everything they need, even if it's at our expense.

Now, this may not be everyone's plight. You may be fortunate enough to truly have it all together and have come to terms with how to keep all the balls in the air and your mind intact. But some of us, and yes, I said 'Us,' struggle from time to time with the various aspects of the life we live and the roles we have to play.

Hats can be easily put on and taken off, and we can slip in and out life's roles as needed. Those two things alone can be assets when you are navigating and maneuvering through life. In either case, the man in the mirror is still recognizable. But I think the mask is a different story. You aren't recognized behind the mask. You can become someone else behind the mask. The problem is, it can become so much a part of you that it becomes difficult to remove. The real you, the God designed you, is now on the verge of becoming lost and completely confused, or ceremoniously stuck when it comes to any revelatory knowledge about your divine purpose. You may even find yourself in a place you were never meant to be and doing what you were never meant to do. Whether this makes sense to you right now or not, keep reading. Somewhere in these pages you will have a moment that will inspire you to better understand how to maintain the balance in your life that you desire, and God intended without ever having to hide behind the mask. Make sense? Then let's proceed with an overview of the four overarching categories at the forefront:

Relationships
Professional
Social
Church

MAYBE I DO, MAYBE I DON'T

I enter into relationships cautiously
but with an open mind
refusing to hold present relationships
hostage to past experiences.
Andrea L. Hines
(When Life Speaks)

Ah, relationships. Here is where you find people hiding, most often, in plain sight. People want to be what you want them to be in order to preserve the feelings they have for one another. They can be found in friends who become lovers, parent to child, employee to employer, professor to student—you name it and some of the same attributes and challenges will possibly surface. Too often we are willing to sacrifice the better part of ourselves to 'make it work.' You compromise your 'deal breakers' here and there for the sake of keeping the relationship alive. Bad move. I believe they will help to ground you and solidify who you really are, not who you want to appear to be, so know them before your relationships begin.

When deal breakers have been established before the relationship was on your radar, you are less likely to make allowances and excuses. Once your feelings are involved, you tend to begin to adjust and start to give the deal breaker a makeover insisting that perhaps the thing you would never put up with isn't really that bad after all. All relationships are important and whenever they're broken the after-effects can be devastating and healing seems almost impossible.

For right now, I want to speak specifically

to the relationship that often takes us down the proverbial aisle to happily-ever-after, at least that's what we hope for and look forward to. It begins with the simple phrase, "I'm Getting Married."

These few words can forever change the lives of those who announce it or friends and family who have patiently waited to hear what they hope and pray is good news. This one may not be as cut and dry as the roles we play, but I'm going to do what I can to share what I've learned to make this less complicated.

Marriage is not just a commitment to your partner, but a journey in building a life together as one. Different roles and different hats in the marriage journey can be anticipated and not necessarily harmful. The mask on the other hand can definitely carry the title of what not to wear.

Little girls dream of the day they can flash the ring, share the phrase, pick the gown before they have a mate in mind, and plan the biggest day of their lives. Not so with boys. I do know that young men often begin to envision being husbands and fathers when they begin to see their peers making that walk down the aisle. Age can create a certain amount of pressure as biological clocks begin to tick and inquiring minds begin to ask, "What are you waiting for?" Primary hats worn by the happy couple are those of bread winner/provider, maintaining the household, and if children are involved, proper parenting. What gets us into trouble is this very hazy picture of the white picket fence, 2.5 angelic children, well-loved pets, continuous opportunities for advancement, zero financial problems, and of course, a sex life of intimacy, romance, and trips to the moon and back. That would all be great if it was real rather than rare.

As a certified life coach, whenever I talk to those who have jumped the broom and have become unhappy, or restless, I'm always surprised at how life issues that are important to both parties were never fully and honestly disclosed before the happy couple said, "I do." Unfortunately, that can come about with or without the benefit of pre-marital counseling. People become more concerned with giving responses that they think the other person wants to hear rather than realizing they are traditional making decisions or giving responses that will set them up or pull them down for a lifetime. You marry and discover the love of your life wants a career over kids, or they attended church because you attended church but have no relationship with God. How do you miss those things?

For whatever reason, I've seen people enter into some relationships knowing the truth and convincing themselves that "she doesn't really mean that," or "he'll change his mind once we've been together awhile."

Newsflash: you can't change anybody. The other person is not going to change his/her mind and decide to do or be what YOU want rather than what THEY want just to make you happy. It might be a shock, but no one is responsible for your happiness but you, and so it begins. Your community of friends, family and associates are all watching. Day-by-day, you discover you're no longer on the love boat. You're more like two ships passing in the night.

You don't want anyone to know there's agony and unhappiness behind the smiles. Sometimes there's domestic violence and addictive behavior which seems to manifest in many situations where we're living very different private lives from what most people see in public.

Couples stay together without getting help for any number of reasons: they don't want to air the dirty laundry; counseling is canceled because "no one is going to tell me how to run my life and my household;' one partner is so consumed with making the other partner successful, they forget who they are as individuals or what they really want out of life; they stay for the sake of the children who, while they love both parents would rather see them separated and happy than together and miserable.

Just a side note, children are a lot smarter than we think or realize. Deceit, mistrust, lies, excuses, etc. often result when marital bliss becomes a battlefield. Hiding and being dishonest with oneself along with painting a pretty picture that doesn't resemble the truth can leave individuals hurt and broken. It can create emotional breakdowns in a way that causes a chain of pain and a cycle that affects future relationships and generations. As they say, hurting people hurt people and while help is needed it's not always sought. The marital mask is, in my opinion, one of the most difficult and deceptive to master and one of the most damaging masks to wear.

A SEAT AT THE TABLE

To be yourself
in a world that is constantly trying
to make you something else
is the greatest accomplishment.
Ralph Waldo Emerson

When I think about dealing with an individual's professional life, I always have to qualify whether we are talking about a job or a career. To me they are very different. If I simply need a paycheck so I can take care of my bills and put food on the table, I'm not going to have the same drive and/or company concern as someone who is climbing the corporate ladder. Not to mention the entrepreneur who wants to turn their passion into profit, something that will one day replace their 9:00 – 5:00. What will you do to keep the contract, pacify the resource, and make the connection?

No matter which umbrella you find yourself sitting under, the goal will put you in difference spaces and different places with different people. None of the professional choices you make should put you at a place of operating with a 'good enough' mentality as opposed to working in excellence; or lacking integrity; even compromising your values and ethics. It's vital not to devalue who you are for the sake of a dollar. Eventually you will not only dislike what you once loved; you will also lose confidence because of the person you've become.

Depending on the progressive plan of where you want to be and when, you may find yourself being quieter in the workplace than at the PTA meeting, or more forceful than you were as head of the hospitality committee at church. Being able to shift and adjust depending on the circumstance is a great skill and the work environment will test that skill on a daily basis. As with any other scenario, it's important that you can be comfortable with the adjustments you make and don't find yourself completely out of character. Climbing the ladder can put you in questionable circumstances with every rung. Sometimes the choices you have to make can be career altering and sometimes career ending.

Bullying is present on the job just as it was when you were in the third grade. However, knowing how to handle those situations are even more important as an adult. If you're a movie buff, the film 'The Devil Wears Prada' starring Meryl Streep is a perfect example of how the work environment can affect your character, even alter your personality. You may find yourself in a place of not only evaluating the cost of success but also weighing whether or not that cost is worth the consequences.

Whatever hat you have to wear, whatever your title is or your responsibilities include, at the end of the day you should still feel good about who you are and what you do. If that's not the case, you may have to make some changes you weren't anticipating. Promotions may be great for your prosperity plan, but if they rob you of your peace, you will need to know how to readjust.

The 'Me Too Movement' is an exceptional example of what can happen if truth is hidden and masks are worn when it comes to issues of sexual abuse, sexual harassment, and rape culture, particularly but not exclusively in the workplace.

"Who will believe me if I come forward?"

"Will anyone trust me if the allegations are not upheld?"

"Will I carry the stigma for the rest of my life?"

The scenarios from the movement show how important advocates and allies are when these masks are removed, and they should be.

The professional world will come with its own unique levels of stress and all of us deal with stress in different ways, particularly in the moment. That temporary stressful situation may cause you to react in a variety of ways that are not like you. The automatic conclusion is perhaps you're just not having a very good day. Going along to get along; pretending and bending your standards; allowing others to cross the line; failing to make your boundaries clear can all be indicators that trouble, and trauma might be brewing. When what used to be temporary becomes a regular routine, you've traded the hat you so easily used to take on and off, for the mask that will prevent you from becoming who you are really meant to be.

DOWN TIME

If you just set out to be liked,
you would be prepared to compromise
on anything at any time and you would
achieve nothing.
Margaret Thatcher

Down time does not necessarily fall into
any of the other characterizations, but it is
an area that can cause you to create a
persona unlike any of the others. This day
and age we are more aware of the
importance of balance in our lives and
being sure to take time for self-care. It was
only when I took my first plane ride did I
understand the importance of "me first." I
always thought I had to take care of
everyone else before taking care of myself.
I discovered if I put myself last, I would not
have the capacity to take care of anyone

else. Case closed. I get it. The challenge comes when you wait too long to take care of yourself or you've been running on empty so long, when there is time for down time, you have a tendency to let go, and I mean really let go. Here's what I mean: if I'm a sports enthusiast, I may become more competitive, and that spirit of competition may unleash some behavior that I'm not particularly fond of and neither is anyone else.

Self-care of a massage, a manicure and a pedicure, staycation or vacation, can be great for rejuvenating and refreshing. However, it is sometimes used to mask the fact that the need to get away is hiding a deeper issue than "me time."

Clearly everyone needs a break, but you can't lose yourself or put yourself in a position where the hat you wear in your me time can't be found on your resume. The down time could also put you at a place of wanting to do something totally out of character from your usual everyday going-through-the-motions life. Think it not strange to find yourself wanting to be in surroundings frequented by more members of the opposite sex, more time at the gym or Karaoke club where you can engage in "harmless" flirtation. Those things could move up on your list of things to do for relaxation and excitement.

Sometimes people will have a beer or two, or something stronger, to have what they consider a little more freedom. Every now and then may feel like it's OK. Yet when every now and then turns into a pattern that in no way mirrors the identifiable you, that's a warning that things may be getting out of control.

The identifiable you is the person your friends and acquaintances would describe if your name came up in conversation. They are the traits most often associated with who you are. Oh Frank, well he's about six feet tall, muscular, infectious laugh, fun guy. Or You know Phyllis she's a little heavy, short hair, classy dresser, you know the one. But when Frank and Phyllis have a little too much fun at the party, loose language, a little too sexy at the company outing, that's a problem. When they are given attributes not in keeping with the traits you know and you are unable to defend their behavior with "no, that couldn't have been..." down-time has become the place you don't want to admit you ever visited. It's not a hat you want to wear; it's the one you want to pull way down over your eyes so no one will know it's you.

All of us have probably had (or just might be) the friend or family member who is avoided when they are having a little too much fun. They may become abusive, combative, sorrowful or pass out invitations to their pity party already in progress. Their behavior will result in you distancing yourself from them and the drama created by their failure to remember one thing about it. Relationships have been ruined beyond repair when the life of the party turns out to be wearing their mask of choice. Being the social butterfly sounds good, but if it takes you completely out of character you have donned a mask with the makings of those worn by Mardi Gras royalty. Unless you're on Bourbon Street in New Orleans, trust me, that is not a mask you want to wear.

LET THE CHURCH SAY AMEN

The Church is God's idea and a priority
plan for the believer.
Unknown

I don't think there is any place that requires
or encourages doing more than one thing at
a time and living in multi-tasking moments
than the church. But let's take a step back for
a minute. If you believe in God and believe
that He is creator of all things, that He is
sovereign, omnipotent and omnipresent, you
probably also believe that He gave his only
begotten son to be crucified, to die for our
sins. You believe that He rose from the dead,
that we were bought with a price, and the gift
of salvation is given to all willing to receive
it. Jesus brought about the fulfillment of the

Father's plan for the church, a place to gather and worship that was birthed on the day of Pentecost. I encourage you to study how the church came to be. My assignment is to delve into why this amazing God idea has become a place to hide who we really are under the guise of being what we determine God wants us to be by His Word.

We love Him and we need Him whether we want to recognize it or not. There are needs everywhere and since God said He would supply all our need according to His riches in glory, it makes perfect sense to seek Him in what we believe to be His house. Those who believe we exist for His good pleasure and are committed to following and serving Him will sometimes find themselves in a position of overload. Mainly because somewhere down the line we became convinced that doing God's will and His work meant being all things, to all people, all the time.

It's not that we want to stop; sometimes we don't know how to stop or cut back on "the work" without feeling guilty for not having fulfilled what is expected. We serve to the point of exhaustion and often frustration which truly diminishes our ability to reflect the light and love of Christ We are on the usher board, deaconate, trustees, hospitality, Pastor's Aid, music ministry, finance committee and the list goes on and on. Each department (or ministry) has a different dynamic and that dynamic often creates scenarios that cause us to behave within the walls of the church building in a totally different manner than how we behave at home or in the workplace. This is the area where flaws are not allowed, at least that's what we often think.

We hide our true feelings, our short comings, our fatigue, our places of emptiness or the burdens we bear. Why? Because we are servants of the Most High God. We have made the term Christian / believer synonymous with whipping-post or doormat. If you consider yourself someone who loves God, you may have been mistreated in some way and expected to accept abuse as you are questioned with "I thought you said you were a Christian?" We get to a point where we have twisted "sacrifice" into something I don't think God ever intended it to be. Our priorities become skewed, and things go lacking that God never intended to go lacking like our family obligations and even our health, mental and physical. We have to be at church early; we can't miss rehearsal; we need to stay late; we become a committee of one when we don't trust anyone else to come alongside us and assist; we have to pray for the people, visit the sick, feed the hungry, etc. It's not that these things are wrong but if they are out of balance, we could be at a perilous point. This is where we really get into trouble.

Too often if the hats you wear and the roles you play become more than you can handle, you don't want to tell anyone. After all, you are the church. You can handle anything. You dare not get tired. You can't be weary in well doing. You have to work while it is day. You have to pray your way through. Did you fast? Did you seek His face? You must be doing something wrong. Have you identified and repented for the sins you may have committed? You can find scripture after scripture to make you feel like you cannot exercise your right to participate as a member of one of the most overlooked ministries in the church, the ministry of NO. If you're not careful you will also find yourself in a place where a yes with a wrong attitude becomes a no in disguise.

Believers are servants of the Most High God and human beings as well. We forget Romans 8:1 Therefore, there is now no condemnation for those who are in Christ

Jesus, who walk not after the flesh but after the Spirit. We can be fragile, and we can fail, but God still loves us. Unfortunately, you will find those who wear the church mask too afraid or ashamed to admit they need assistance; and too prideful to acknowledge their faults and flaws. They often feel abandoned, disgraced, end up trusting no one and feeling like there is no place to turn. The good news is you don't have to remain behind the mask. You can get help, the right help, and you should. Your survival depends on it. Amen? Amen...

IN CONCLUSION

If we are true to ourselves,
we cannot be false to anyone.
William Shakespeare

I had a conversation with someone I deeply admired and respected. We were talking about how difficult it is for people to seek emotional and mental help regardless of how much they may need it. We came to the conclusion that everyone struggles at some point in their journey to be the best that they can be to not be totally honest with where they really are. Social media has allowed us to perpetuate pseudo celebrity status by likes, clicks, camera angles and algorithms that basically make us look better than we are, depending on your perspective. But real life doesn't look like Facebook, Tik Tok, or Instagram. Real life can look like an emotional roller coaster that you ride more frequently than you want to. You ride because someone dared you. You ride because you don't want to admit you're afraid. You ride because even when you refuse to get a ticket, someone will get one for you because they refuse to accept your objections or limitations.

As our conversation continued, we looked at a variety of mental health statistics and rising suicide numbers. The questions were always the same, "Why didn't they get help?" "Why didn't they just talk to someone?" Easier said than done. Sometimes it's because people don't want to admit their struggle. They don't want you to go behind the Wizard of Oz curtain and discover what you see is not what you get. The sad reality is sometimes when attempts are made to open up, the concerns are dismissed as "You're just having a bad day," "The enemy is attacking, just pray more." or "God's testing you." And since God won't put more on you than you can bear; if you can't withstand the light affliction, you feel as if you have failed. So where does that leave you? Broken, bleeding, isolated, and in a painful place that no one understands.

People tend to treat you without sensitivity when they perceive you're strong and you can take the blows. They don't know you cried all night because the front you've skillfully crafted is coming apart at the seams. They have no idea that you meticulously maintain the mask because you fear what people would say, or do, if they really knew the truth.

I wrote this in hopes that someone will be willing to give and receive the grace needed to continue on a path of self-love realizing they matter just the way they are. That is not to say that we shouldn't all grow and embrace change in the process. It is to say that flaws can be expected and should be accepted without condemnation or judgment.

The masks of life are not only inevitable, but they can also be powerful and purposeful. They are not meant for you to hide behind; worn to cover what you are afraid to confront; or created as an alter ego to take center stage of your life. They should be temporary adjustments and not permanent solutions. You can only own the power of the mask BY REMOVING IT!

My prayer is that you will read these pages with a renewed desire to see yourself as God sees you—whole and complete, fearfully, and wonderfully made. Only then will your mirror image be of the God-sent, God-centered, God-designed reflection that He sees—destiny driven, with purpose personified, unashamed, and without apology. That's when you know you have become a true master of the mask.

ABOUT THE
AUTHOR

Andrea L. Hines
*Mother, Grandmother, Author, Poet, Speaker,
Entrepreneur, Doctor of Divinity, Certified Life
Coach and Radio Host*

This lady of many talents is a native of Washington, D.C. who now resides in Raleigh, North Carolina. She often says that moving to the "quiet beauty of the Carolinas" deepened her relationship with God and caused her creativity to flow freely.

Andrea has over thirty years of experience in the performing arts as an actor, playwright, and director, with performances in numerous community theater and film projects. She has been a narrator for the North Carolina Library for the Blind and Physically Handicapped; and continues to enjoy lending her voice to any number of voice-over projects.

Her poetic work has been featured in local newspapers, on Blue Mountain Arts greeting cards and products, and included in numerous anthologies. She has written a collection of inspirational verses titled 'When He Whispers', words of encouragement inspired by her granddaughter titled, 'Nanny Nuggets'; and inspiration through affirmations – When Life Speaks, You Speak Life. While Andrea has authored story poems, greeting cards and other works, she says God has given her the ability to write the words people often think but can't express.

She introduced her company, A's Accents in 1994. Her performance and product showcase, "…A Work in Progress.," weaves a story of life experiences through her original verses with musical interludes. "A Reading for His Glory" provides a more intimate atmosphere with smaller groups, giving them the opportunity to interact with the author on a more personal level. Her style and ability to uplift the heart has made her a favorite speaker in areas from commencement exercises to conferences. You can see her on her You Tube channel – Andrea L. Hines – and hear her as she hosts programs on her own internet radio/TV station, ALH Broadcasting, an affiliate of SIBN – Streaming Inspirational Broadcast Network.

Andrea has received an honorary Doctorate Degree of Divinity and also serves as an Elder at The River Church in Durham, North Carolina. She is a Certified Life Coach, and owner of C.L.A.S.S Coaching and Consulting-Cultivating Lives and Success Strategies. She believes God has blessed her with certain gifts, and only hopes that whatever she creates will be to His glory and a blessing to someone else.

www.ingramcontent.com/pod-product-compliance
Lightning Source LLC
Chambersburg PA
CBHW070944120626
46546CB00004B/1560

* 9 7 8 1 9 5 4 8 1 8 4 0 8 *